DK SUPER History

GEORGE WASHINGTON AND THE AMERICAN REVOLUTION

Learn all about George Washington, Founding Father and first president of the US, and his role in the history of America

PRODUCED FOR DK BY
Editorial Just Content Limited
Design Studio Noel

Author Ann Weil

Senior Editor Ankita Awasthi Tröger
Editor Hattie Hansford
Senior Art Editor Gilda Pacitti
Graphic Story Illustrator Matt Garbutt
Managing Editor Carine Tracanelli
Managing Art Editor Sarah Corcoran
Pre-Production Coordinator Shanker Prasad
Pre-Production Designer Jaypal Chauhan
Production Controller Rebecca Parton
Publisher Sarah Forbes
Managing Director, Learning Hilary Fine

First published in Great Britain in 2025 by
Dorling Kindersley Limited
20 Vauxhall Bridge Road,
London SW1V 2SA

The authorised representative in the EEA is
Dorling Kindersley Verlag GmbH. Arnulfstr. 124,
80636 Munich, Germany

10 9 8 7 6 5 4 3 2 1
001–350113–Sep/2025

A CIP catalogue record for this book
is available from the British Library.
ISBN: 978-0-2417-4472-7

Printed and bound in China

www.dk.com

This book was made with Forest Stewardship Council™ certified paper – one small step in DK's commitment to a sustainable future.
Learn more at www.dk.com/uk/information/sustainability

Contents

Words in **bold** are explained in the glossary on page 44.

History in Perspective

George Washington had a huge impact on the United States during his life and after his death. As a young soldier, he fought alongside other colonists for Great Britain in their war against France. As the leader of the **Continental Army**, he led troops and defeated Great Britain in the American Revolution. Later, he became the first president of the United States of America.

Lots of people made an impact on Washington, and his life and actions also affected several individuals, groups and countries.

In 1789, Washington was **elected** the first president of the United States. He led the new United States for two **terms**.

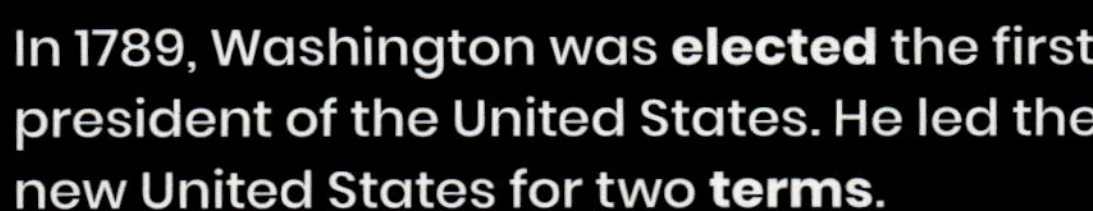

Where and when?

George Washington was born in 1732 in Virginia, where he spent most of his life. For the first year and a half of his presidency, he was based in New York. He then **relocated** to Philadelphia, Pennsylvania, when the **government** moved the capital there. In 1791, **Congress** named Washington, DC after him. He died in Virginia in 1799.

Before he became a politician, Washington was a skilled soldier who fought in many battles.

Think about it

What kinds of **sources** could we use to learn about George Washington?

Who was involved?

There were many important people in Washington's life, including the family he grew up with in Virginia, the family he later raised at Mount Vernon and the **enslaved** people who worked for him. Other important figures include the British military leaders he reported to as a young soldier and the troops he led to victory as commander of the Continental Army. He fought alongside **Indigenous** peoples in some battles, while in others he faced them as enemies. Today, he is considered one of the **Founding Fathers** of the United States. He was also the country's first president.

Different perspectives

Different groups in society may have deeply contrasting experiences of events. Official records of the past often only present one side of the story. This means that they can't reflect the experiences of everyone affected. To understand what happened, it is important that we look at events from more than one point of view.

Key Events

WHAT HAPPENED WHEN

George Washington played a crucial role in shaping the United States into what it is today. He led the Continental Army, defeating the British and creating a new country. As the first US president, he made important rules for running the nation. He is commonly known as the "father of his country" because he helped develop American **democracy**.

1732

22 FEBRUARY

Washington is born on a tobacco **plantation** in the **colony** of Virginia.

1752

MAY

Washington joins the Virginia **militia**.

1754

24 MAY

Washington leads British colonial troops in an attack on a French fort. The fort is built on land claimed by both Great Britain and France. Washington is forced to surrender. This sparks the beginning of the **French and Indian War**, which is part of the larger **Seven Years' War** between Great Britain and France.

1759

6 JANUARY

Washington marries Martha Dandridge Custis, a wealthy 26-year-old widow. She has a son and daughter from her first marriage.

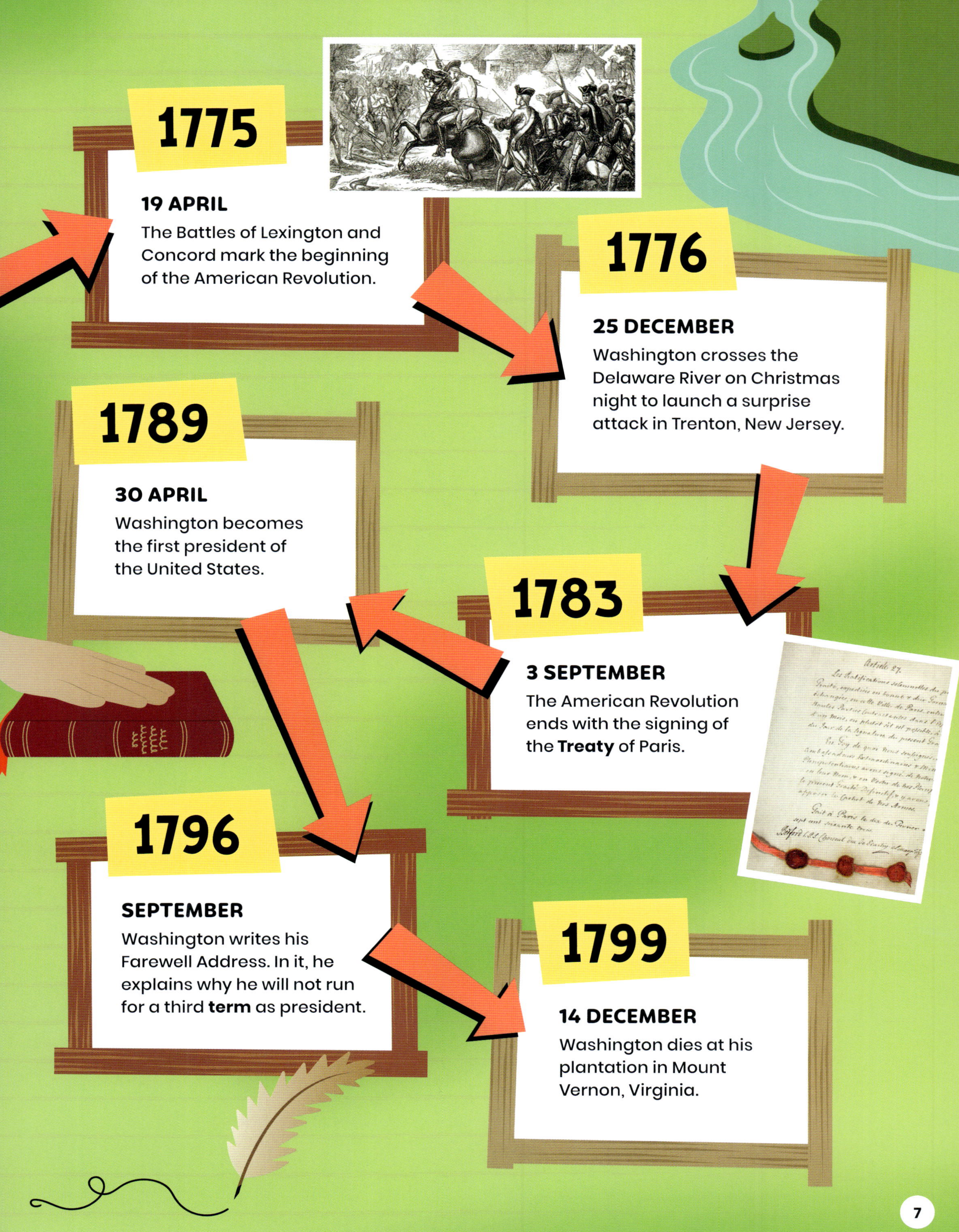

1775

19 APRIL

The Battles of Lexington and Concord mark the beginning of the American Revolution.

1776

25 DECEMBER

Washington crosses the Delaware River on Christmas night to launch a surprise attack in Trenton, New Jersey.

1783

3 SEPTEMBER

The American Revolution ends with the signing of the **Treaty** of Paris.

1789

30 APRIL

Washington becomes the first president of the United States.

1796

SEPTEMBER

Washington writes his Farewell Address. In it, he explains why he will not run for a third **term** as president.

1799

14 DECEMBER

Washington dies at his plantation in Mount Vernon, Virginia.

Key People
WHO'S WHO

George Washington lived a long and full life, from his time on his father's plantation to serving as the first president of the United States. Here are some of the key people in this story.

Political leaders

Benjamin Franklin

Benjamin Franklin
One of the Founding Fathers of the United States. He helped draft the **Declaration of Independence** and was one of the people who signed the US **Constitution**.

John Adams
A **Founding Father** who helped write the Declaration of Independence and also helped **negotiate** the Treaty of Paris.

John Jay
A Founding Father who Washington appointed to be the first chief justice of the **Supreme Court**.

Alexander Hamilton
A Founding Father who helped write the US Constitution. He served as the first secretary of the Cabinet under George Washington.

James Madison
A Founding Father and the main author of the US Constitution.

Thomas Jefferson
A Founding Father and the main author of the Declaration of Independence. He later became the third president of the United States.

Benjamin Tallmadge

Military leaders

Edward Braddock
A British commander who served in the French and Indian War.

Charles Cornwallis
The leader of the British Army who surrendered at the Battle of Yorktown.

Count Rochambeau and Count de Grasse
French military leaders who commanded French troops at the Battle of Yorktown.

Benjamin Tallmadge
An American military officer who led the Culper Spy Ring.

Family

Augustine Washington
Washington's father. He passed away suddenly when George was 11 years old.

Mary Ball Washington
Washington's mother. She had six children with Augustine and raised them alone after he died.

Martha Dandridge Custis
Washington's wife. They married in 1759 and were together for 40 years.

John Parke Custis and Martha Parke Custis
Nicknamed Jacky and Patsy, they were Washington's stepchildren.

Martha Dandridge Custis

Key Location
MOUNT VERNON

Mount Vernon was George Washington's **estate** and where he lived for most of his life. The estate was very important to him and he used his connection to the land as inspiration in his speeches. It represented his ideals about independence, self-sufficiency and hard work. His decision to leave Mount Vernon and lead his troops during the war demonstrated his deep commitment to those same ideals. Despite his fame after the war, Washington returned to Mount Vernon instead of seeking more power or money. This reinforced his reputation as a leader who believed in acting for the people, rather than for his own ambitions.

By the time of Washington's death in 1799, the Mount Vernon estate covered well over 32 sq km (12 sq miles). This included formal gardens, forests and lots of **fertile** farmland that was for good for growing crops and supporting livestock.

After his death in December 1799, Washington was buried in a family tomb at Mount Vernon. His will left instructions for a new brick tomb to be built to replace the original one. In 1831, his body was moved there, along with the remains of his wife, Martha, and other family members.

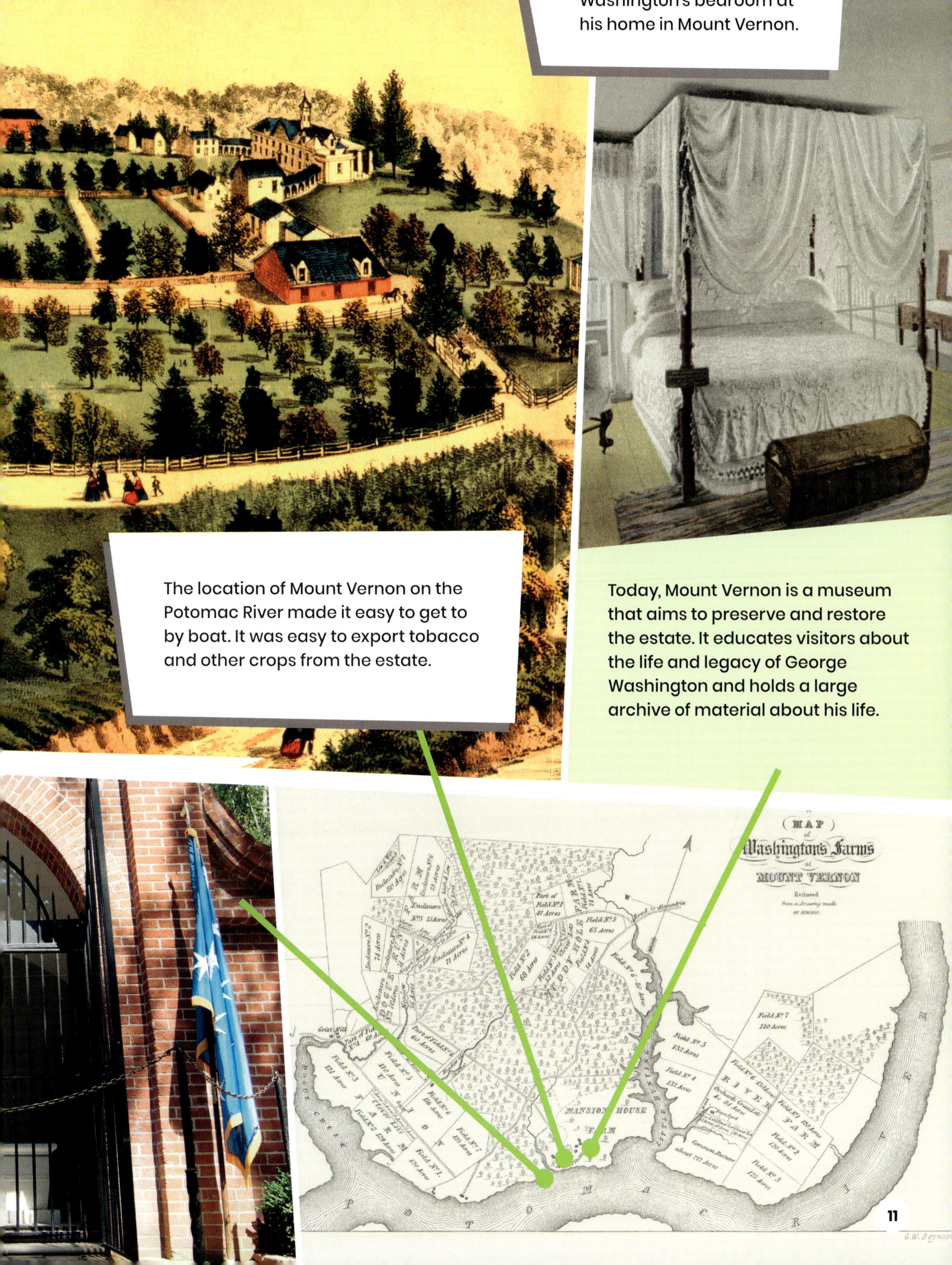

Washington's bedroom at his home in Mount Vernon.

The location of Mount Vernon on the Potomac River made it easy to get to by boat. It was easy to export tobacco and other crops from the estate.

Today, Mount Vernon is a museum that aims to preserve and restore the estate. It educates visitors about the life and legacy of George Washington and holds a large archive of material about his life.

Growing Up in Virginia

George Washington was born in 1732 on a tobacco plantation in Popes Creek, Virginia. Virginia was one of the British colonies. The area had rich soil and a warm climate, which made it very good for farming. Wealthy **planters**, such as Washington's father, owned most of the land and had a lot of power. Many of the workers who helped grow and pick the crops on the land were enslaved.

John Washington, George's great-grandfather, settled down at Popes Creek in the mid-1600s. In the 1720s, George's father Augustine built a home there.

Augustine Washington owned several plantations. George Washington's mother, Mary Ball Washington, was Augustine's second wife. George was the first of their six children.

In the early 1600s, some Indigenous peoples were forced into **slavery** in Virginia. Poor people from Great Britain came to work on farms as **indentured** servants. By the late 1600s, most workers on tobacco farms were enslaved African people. They were forcibly taken from their homes and sold to the British.

When Washington was six years old, his family moved to another plantation. It was called Ferry Farm.

Washington was very young when his father passed away. As a child, he admired him. This picture shows them together.

A DEATH IN THE FAMILY

When Washington was 11 years old, his father died suddenly. While Washington's older half brothers attended school in England, he could not do the same after his father's death because the family had less money. Washington continued to live at Ferry Farm with his mother and younger brothers and sisters. His mother never remarried. Instead of going to school, Washington learned how to run the tobacco plantation. He studied subjects like **geometry** at home. This helped prepare him for his first job as a land **surveyor**.

Land surveying was a respected career. However, Washington felt **embarrassed** about his lack of education for most of his life. This picture shows him at work.

Fascinating fact

Washington was largely self-taught. He learned by reading books and studying on his own. He was very curious and wanted to know as much as he could.

From Surveyor to Soldier

In 1749, George Washington got an important job as surveyor of Culpepper County, Virginia. He was just 17 years old. The job involved measuring and mapping areas to help people figure out where they could build homes and settle. Around this time, France was claiming land it had been sharing with Great Britain. So, like both his grandfathers, Washington decided to join the Virginia militia in 1752.

The next year, the governor of Virginia sent him on an important mission to talk to the French troops. Washington made a difficult journey across the mountains to the Ohio River Valley. He travelled there with another surveyor named Christopher Gist and some men who carried their equipment. Washington's orders were to demand that the French Army leave.

Washington's role as surveyor helped him learn a lot about the land. It was a skill that would be very useful to him later in his life.

THE BATTLE OF FORT NECESSITY

In 1752, Washington became a **major** in the Virginia **Regiment**, fighting for Great Britain. In 1754, Washington's troops ran into a group of French soldiers and a fight broke out. A French officer was killed, although Washington had not planned an attack. His troops were not ready for battle – they were **outnumbered**. They retreated to a small fort they had built called Fort Necessity. Washington was forced to surrender there. He signed a paper saying he was guilty of killing the French officer. After this, Washington decided to **resign**.

The next year, Major General Edward Braddock travelled from Great Britain to lead an army against the French troops.

THE BATTLE OF THE MONONGAHELA

In February 1755, British Major General Edward Braddock came to Virginia. Having reflected on what happened at Fort Necessity, George Washington saw this as a chance to rejoin the military. He asked to be part of Braddock's team. Braddock accepted and Washington returned to Ohio with the army. There were about 2,400 men carrying lots of heavy weapons. This slowed them down. Near the Monongahela River, Braddock's troops were cornered by French soldiers. The battle was fierce and lasted three hours.

Many British soldiers were hurt or killed in the Battle of the Monongahela. Braddock himself was badly wounded.

Fascinating fact

Washington wrote to his mother after the Battle of the Monongahela, telling her that he had not been harmed, even though he had two horses shot from under him and found four bullet holes in his coat.

The Birth of an Idea

As George Washington started his army career, the American colonies faced new challenges. The French and Indian War made the American colonists think about working together to protect themselves. This was a very important time in the history of the colonies and in Washington's life.

THE ALBANY CONGRESS

In 1754, the British Government told the leaders of the colonies to meet in Albany, New York. They needed to plan their defence against the French. Benjamin Franklin led the Pennsylvania **delegation**. He had an idea to create a new government that would join all the colonies together.

Although eventually it did not happen, Franklin's plan was important – it was the first time the colonists had seriously considered one government.

Franklin published this cartoon in his newspaper, the *Pennsylvania Gazette*, in 1754. It became a famous **symbol** for **unity** among the colonies.

THE 1763 TREATY OF PARIS

The Treaty of Paris was signed in 1763. It marked the end of the French and Indian War. France gave up the **territories** it had claimed in North America. This was an important victory for Great Britain. The Treaty of Paris gave Britain control of all French land east of the Mississippi River.

BOSTON TEA PARTY

Washington and other colonial soldiers helped win the war against France. But after the war, Britain introduced new taxes in the colonies on everyday items like sugar and paper. This was to help cover the costs of war. The taxes made the colonists angry. In 1773, a group of colonists known as the Sons of Liberty organised a protest against British taxes and British rule. They dumped 342 chests of valuable tea into Boston Harbor, Massachusetts. This event is known as the Boston Tea Party. In response, King George III passed the Intolerable Acts. These led to the First Continental Congress where delegates met and agreed to boycott British goods if the Intolerable Acts were not revoked by 1 December 1774.

Think about it

What were the main reasons that the American colonists wanted to form their own nation?

A RALLYING CRY FOR REVOLUTION

In March 1775, a politician named Patrick Henry spoke at the Virginia Assembly. He gave an important speech against British taxes. In it, he said the now-famous words, "Give me liberty or give me death!" (Henry and Humphrey, 1913). His speech inspired many people to fight for their freedom. It became a **rallying cry** for the American Revolution.

Home Life at Mount Vernon

Amidst his political and military duties, George Washington also made time for leisure and social activities at home. He inherited the Mount Vernon estate from his half brother, Lawrence, in 1761. His experience as a surveyor helped him find **unclaimed** land nearby. Over time, Washington made Mount Vernon much larger.

Washington purchased land from neighbours and found new areas to add to his estate, which he grew to over 32 sq km (12 sq miles).

Fascinating fact

Washington loved to host weekly dinners and parties at the Mount Vernon estate. These social gatherings were also important opportunities to discuss politics.

This engraving shows Washington with his wife, Martha, and his stepchildren.

FAMILY LIFE

Washington married Martha Dandridge Custis in 1759. They did not have any children of their own. Washington adored his two stepchildren, John Parke Custis and Martha Parke Custis. John was nicknamed Jacky when he was young. Martha was nicknamed Patsy.

Patsy had serious health problems and died when she was 17 years old. Jacky married a woman named Nelly and had seven children. He died in 1781 from a sickness he got in the camps during the Battle of Yorktown. After Jacky's death, George and Martha raised his children at Mount Vernon.

Washington enjoyed farming the land at Mount Vernon.

FARMER

Although he had no formal education, Washington had privately studied **agriculture**. He put what he learned into practice at Mount Vernon. At first, he grew tobacco. Then, he switched to wheat as his **cash crop**. He rotated crops on his five farms and tried different ways to keep the soil fertile. He also kept dairy cows to supply his large extended family with milk, butter and cream, and sold the produce that was left over.

DOG LOVER

Washington loved animals, especially dogs. There were a variety of different **breeds** of dogs at Mount Vernon. Some were pets that belonged to different members of the family. Washington also helped develop a breed of dog known as the American Foxhound.

Washington enjoyed being home with his family and working on his projects. But in 1775, he left his beloved Mount Vernon to travel to Philadelphia, Pennsylvania. There, he represented Virginia at the **Second Continental Congress**.

Declaring Independence

The desire for independence had not faded. Tensions between the colonists and British **authorities** continued to grow. Neither side seemed willing to back down. In Massachusetts, groups of colonists formed militias. They were ready when British troops marched into the towns of Lexington and Concord, Massachusetts, in April 1775 to take away their weapons. This marked the start of the American Revolution.

Washington designed his own uniform – a blue wool coat with a cream lining, collar, lapels and cuffs. It was sewn by an indentured servant at Mount Vernon.

SECOND CONTINENTAL CONGRESS

In May 1775, after the Battles of Lexington and Concord, **delegates** from each of the 13 colonies met in Philadelphia. This was known as the Second Continental Congress and it served as a temporary government. It printed money, set up the first postal service and managed relations with Indigenous communities. Most importantly, it created the Continental Army. Washington was chosen to be the army's commander. He led the troops for eight years until the end of the American Revolution.

THE CONTINENTAL ARMY

The Continental Army was mostly made up of white men from the 13 colonies. It also included free and enslaved Black men. Occasionally, women helped in battle. Some were spies, but women mostly helped support soldiers – they were **camp followers** who helped cook, nursed the injured and sold supplies.

Deborah Sampson was born in Massachusetts in 1760. She disguised herself as a man to serve in the Continental Army as a soldier. When her commander discovered she was a woman, she was honourably **discharged** from the army. She was the only woman to earn a full military **pension**.

DECLARATION OF INDEPENDENCE

The Second Continental Congress voted for independence on 2 July 1776. Two days later, they released a declaration that explained their reasons. It was mainly written by Thomas Jefferson. Washington did not sign the Declaration of Independence because he was leading troops in New York at the time. He received a copy from John Hancock, the president of Congress. On 9 July, he ordered his soldiers to gather in Manhattan, New York, to hear the declaration read aloud.

The Declaration of Independence stated that all men were made equal, but it did not address slavery and both women and Indigenous people were left out of the declaration.

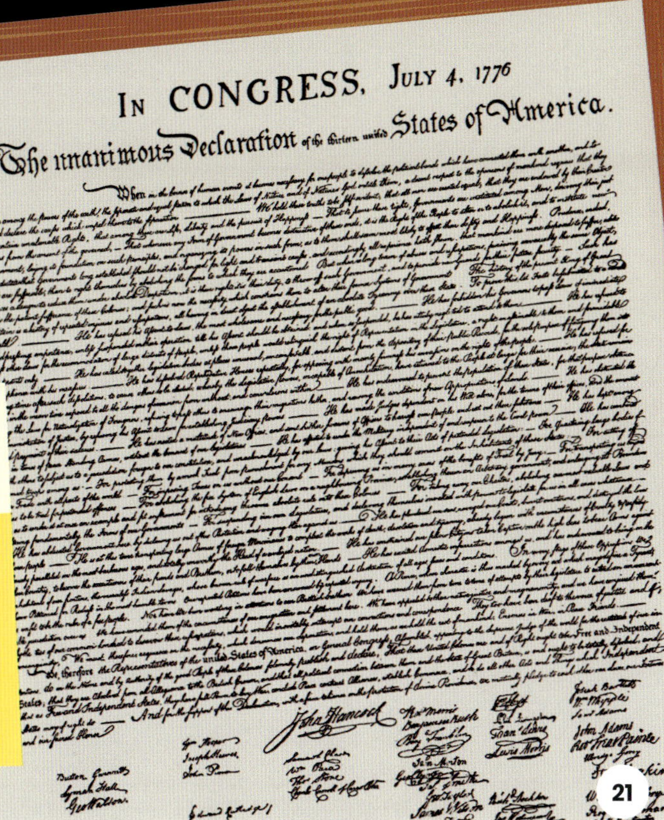

IN CONGRESS, JULY 4, 1776

The unanimous Declaration of the thirteen united States of America.

Fascinating fact

The Declaration of Independence was not signed on 4 July because many delegates were not in Philadelphia at the time. Most of them signed it on 2 August 1776.

A Dangerous Crossing

Soldiers
Members of the Continental Army during the American Revolution

George Washington
Commander in chief of the Continental Army during the American Revolution

Henry Knox
Chief artillery officer of the Continental Army during the American Revolution

Hessian guards
German soldiers fighting on the side of the British Army during the American Revolutic

Christmas night, 1776, on the banks of the Delaware River.

It's so cold, I can't feel my toes!

We must cross the river to Trenton tonight and surprise the enemy.

But General Washington, it's freezing. How will we cross?

We'll use boats. Colonel Knox, are the boats ready?

Yes, sir, but it will be dangerous to cross with this much ice.

The soldiers quickly loaded their boats and prepared for the crossing.
How can we paddle in this weather?
The ice is so thick... we must be careful.
Stay strong, men! Remember what we're fighting for!
The soldiers pushed off into the icy waters.

My hands are freezing - I can hardly feel the oar.
Keep paddling, we're almost there!
The brave soldiers rowed through the cold.
We've made it!
Now, men, let's prepare for our surprise attack!

As dawn broke, Washington led his troops towards Trenton.
What a quiet morning.
Charge!
The surprise attack was a success. Washington's brave crossing had led to victory.
Well done, men! This victory will give hope to our entire nation.

The American Revolution

In December 1776, the Continental Army won a key battle at Trenton, New Jersey. They defeated German soldiers called **Hessians** who were fighting for the British Army. This victory was George Washington's first major success in the American Revolution. It lifted the spirits of his troops and encouraged more men to join the army. In October 1777, at the Battle of Saratoga, the Continental Army forced the British soldiers to surrender.

The Continental Army's victory at the Battle of Saratoga convinced France to join the war. It became a formal **ally** of the American colonists.

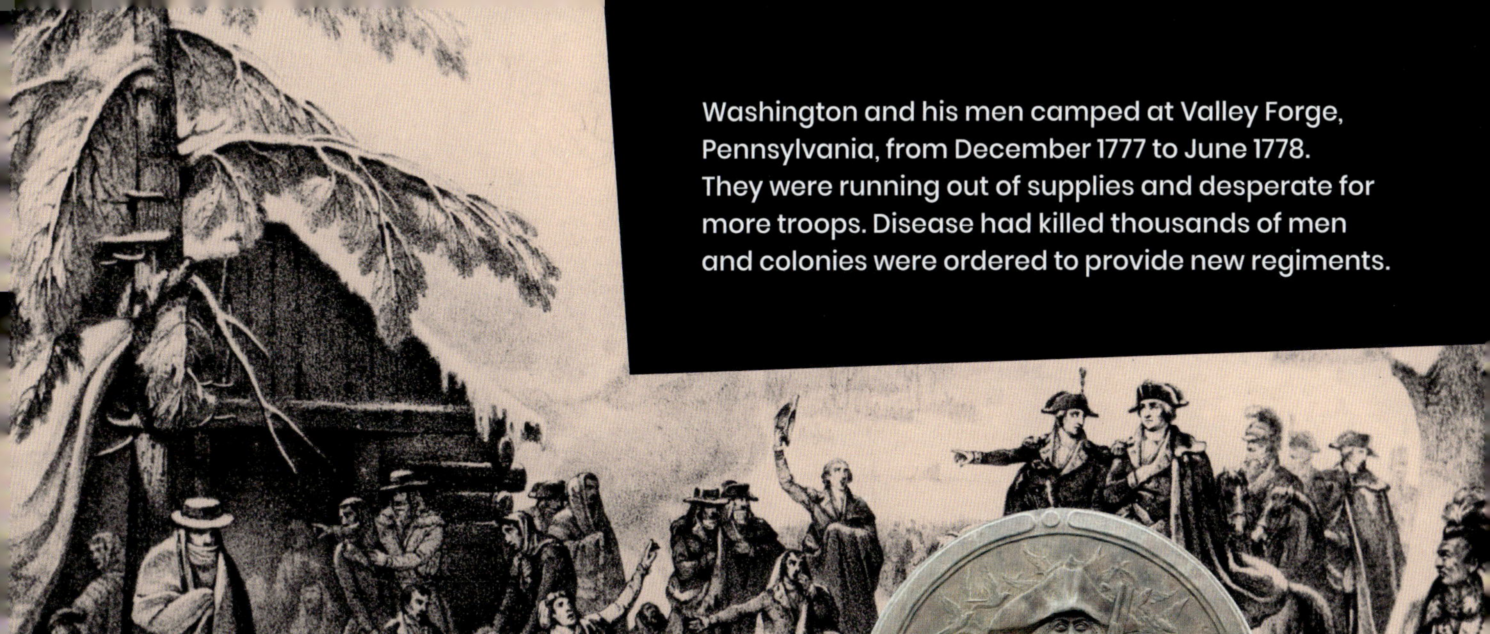

Washington and his men camped at Valley Forge, Pennsylvania, from December 1777 to June 1778. They were running out of supplies and desperate for more troops. Disease had killed thousands of men and colonies were ordered to provide new regiments.

AMERICA'S FIRST BLACK SOLDIERS

Black soldiers were a vital part of the Continental Army. There were around 700 Black soldiers at Valley Forge, mostly from Rhode Island, Connecticut, and Massachusetts. In 1778, Rhode Island leaders decided to let enslaved Black, mixed race and Indigenous men join the army. As a result, the First Rhode Island Regiment became well known for including several Black soldiers. Enslavers did not like this new rule, and Rhode Island took back the offer in June 1778. Nonetheless, by the end, the First Rhode Island Regiment had 144 Black soldiers out of a total of 225 enlisted men.

This monument in Valley Forge National Historical Park honours the Black soldiers who fought in the American Revolution.

THE CULPER SPY RING

The Culper Spy Ring was a secret group of spies who helped the Continental Army during the American Revolution. They worked from 1778 to 1783, mostly in New York City and Long Island, New York, to gather important information about the British Army. Major Benjamin Tallmadge organised the spy ring. The spies used **code** names and clever tricks, such as invisible ink, to send messages without getting caught.

Fascinating fact

Anna Strong played an important role in the Culper Spy Ring. Historians believe she used her clothesline to signal to the group. She would hang out different items of clothing to send different messages.

America's Victory

The Battle of Yorktown was very important in deciding the fate of the American Revolution. It took place in Virginia from 28 September to 19 October 1781. George Washington led his troops with the support of the French Army, led by Count de Grasse and Count Rochambeau. Together, the American and French soldiers attacked the British Army in a battle that lasted 21 days.

John Adams, Benjamin Franklin and John Jay.

PEACE TALKS

On 19 October 1781, General Cornwallis, who led the British troops, surrendered his whole army and ended the Battle of Yorktown. This was the last fight of the American Revolution. After the battle ended, British leaders agreed to talk about ending the war. Peace talks officially started in Paris, France, in 1782. Benjamin Franklin, John Adams and John Jay worked to get the best possible terms for the new United States.

THE 1782 TREATY OF PARIS

On 3 September 1782, the Treaty of Paris was signed at the Hôtel d'York in Paris. The United States of America was officially an independent nation. The treaty defined the boundaries of the new country and gave the United States **territory** east of the Mississippi River. The Treaty of Paris also resolved other issues, like debts from before the war and fishing rights.

WASHINGTON'S RESIGNATION

With the war over, Washington felt his job leading the army was complete. He wanted to return to family life at Mount Vernon. So, on 23 December 1783, he appeared before Congress to resign as commander in chief. Washington's resignation was important. It meant that regular citizens would be in charge of the United States, not the army.

THE CONSTITUTIONAL CONVENTION

The **Articles of Confederation**, established in 1781 as the first constitution of the United States, were not working well. In 1787, delegates from 12 states met in Philadelphia to create a new plan to govern the United States. The group chose Washington to lead their meeting. For four months, they discussed how to make a better government. In the end, they wrote the US Constitution. The constitution was a set of rules for how to run the country. It said that the government would be divided into three parts: one part would make new laws, one would carry out the laws and one would judge the laws. The constitution is still followed today.

Think about it

Why do you think the delegates decided to split the government into three parts?

Washington and His Cabinet

In 1788, the US Constitution became the law of the United States. It set out the need for a strong, central government to run the country. The next year, George Washington was elected the first president of the United States by the **Electoral College**. Washington was **inaugurated** on 30 April 1789, in New York City.

The constitution strengthened the national government. It gave the president important powers, especially in dealing with other countries.

THE PRESIDENT'S ADVISERS

During his first term as president, Washington chose a team of close advisers to support him in running the government. This team was known as the Cabinet of the United States.

Fascinating fact

The term "cabinet" is still used to refer to the US president's closest advisers.

ALEXANDER HAMILTON

After the war, Alexander Hamilton helped write the US Constitution. He is considered one of the Founding Fathers of the United States. When Washington became president, he chose Hamilton to be secretary of the treasury. This important role let Hamilton shape the new country's financial policies. Hamilton had a **Federalist** view. This means that he supported a strong and united central government. His work helped set up financial systems and influenced the direction of the new United States.

Alexander Hamilton

THOMAS JEFFERSON

President Washington named Thomas Jefferson his secretary of state. In this job, Jefferson gave advice on how to deal with other countries. He wanted local communities to have more power to make decisions. He thought farms were more important to the future of the United States than cities. Jefferson and Washington had been close friends for many years, but Jefferson worried that President Washington was becoming too much like a king. Jefferson even criticised Washington publicly for this. This shows how strongly Jefferson felt about keeping the United States from having a ruler like a king.

Thomas Jefferson

Henry Knox

Edmund Randolph

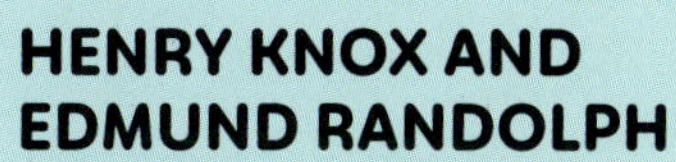

HENRY KNOX AND EDMUND RANDOLPH

Henry Knox and Edmund Randolph were important members of the Cabinet. Both men had fought in the American Revolution and were trusted advisers to Washington. Knox served as secretary of war. He dealt with military affairs and relationships with Indigenous communities. Randolph was the first attorney general. He set up the country's **justice** system.

Building a Nation

Washington picked the location for the nation's government buildings. This included the president's official residence, known today as the White House.

George Washington followed the constitution carefully. He knew the new country needed strong leadership, but he respected the rules put in place to keep the government fair. He chose the first Supreme Court judges and started traditions such as Inauguration Day speeches and State of the Union addresses.

!!!

???

DIFFERENT IDEAS

Washington surrounded himself with advisers who had strong, independent opinions. They included James Madison, Alexander Hamilton and Thomas Jefferson, who often disagreed with each other on economic policies and the role of the federal government.

Washington was very careful in his dealings with other countries. He chose to keep the United States **neutral**. This meant that the United States could focus on growing and building itself without getting pulled into conflicts happening far away.

James Madison

John Adams

JAMES MADISON

James Madison was the main author of the US Constitution. Washington relied on his advice, especially during his first term. Washington asked Madison to write important public speeches for him, including his first inauguration speech. Madison often disagreed with Hamilton. Later, Madison worked with Jefferson to set up the **Republican Party**. They did this to offer an alternative to the Federalists, who had different ideas about how the government should work.

JOHN ADAMS

John Adams was the first vice president of the United States. He ran meetings in the **Senate** and cast 29 tie-breaking votes. That is more than any other US vice president in history. These votes helped shape key laws and decisions at a time when senators were often divided by different political views.

Think about it

Why do you think Washington chose people with different views to work with him?

WASHINGTON STEPS DOWN

On 19 September 1796, after serving two terms as president, George Washington used his Farewell Address to announce his decision to step down. In his speech, he spoke about his decision not to seek a third term and shared his thoughts on the future of the United States. This set an unofficial standard of two terms for the US presidency.

Washington's Farewell Address is read each year in the Senate to remind lawmakers of his warnings and hopes for the nation.

In Washington's Memory

As one of the most important figures in US history, George Washington is remembered in a lot of ways. The US capital, Washington, DC, is named in his honour. The state of Washington is also named after him. In Virginia, a road named in his memory runs along the Potomac River from Mount Vernon.

When it was completed in 1884, the Washington Monument was the tallest building in the world. It was modelled after ancient Egyptian **obelisks**.

Washington is the face of the US dollar bill.

LEGAL HOLIDAY
Washington's Birthday
February 22nd
No Business Transacted
IN PRIN... G CO.,PHILADELPHIA-*Founded in 1728 by Benj. Franklin*-NEW YORK OFFICE, 200 FIFTH AVEN

PRESIDENTS' DAY

Unusually, Americans celebrated Washington's birthday during his lifetime. The celebrations carried on after he died in 1799. In 1879, Congress made Washington's birthday, 22 February, an official national holiday. It was the first federal holiday set up in honour of someone's birthday. In 1968, Congress changed the holiday to the third Monday in February. This was to give workers a three-day weekend. Today, this holiday is known as Presidents' Day.

Think about it

How do **memorials** help us remember people? Why are they important?

The George Washington Memorial Parkway was designed to be a scenic road for people to travel along.

THE GEORGE WASHINGTON MEMORIAL PARKWAY

This scenic road in Virginia opened on 16 January 1932, exactly 200 years after Washington's birth. It is 40 km (25 miles) long and runs along the Potomac River between McLean and Mount Vernon. It links lots of important sites, including different parks and memorials. It was built in sections, with all parts finally open in 1970. Before the road opened, it used to take several hours to travel from Washington, DC to Mount Vernon, but this road cuts it down to only around 30 minutes. In 1929, Congress decided to change the road's name from the Mount Vernon Memorial Parkway to the George Washington Memorial Parkway. The scale of the road and the important sites it links shows how important the memory of George Washington is to America.

The Arlington Memorial Bridge over the Potomac River is part of the George Washington Memorial Parkway.

Lessons from History

George Washington was commander in chief of the military forces that fought for and won American independence. He helped the United States become a free country, and served as its first president. His memory lives on in the military term "commander in chief", which is still used to refer to the president today. So what can we learn from how Washington lived and the choices he made?

CIVIC VIRTUE

Washington always showed civic virtue, which means being a good citizen with strong **morals**. He tried to act for what was best for the country, regardless of his own personal preferences. All through his life, Washington was known for his strong character.

Washington put his own wants aside in order to serve his country, focusing on what was best for everyone. This is important for a democracy to work well.

Fascinating fact

Washington was **posthumously** promoted to the rank of "General of the Armies" in 1976. This means that no future military officer would outrank him.

110 Rules of Civility offers guidelines on how to treat others with respect and kindness. They are still important today because they emphasise good manners, honesty and fairness.

RULES OF CIVILITY

When he was about 14 years old, Washington copied the *110 Rules of Civility* into his school notebook. These guidelines for good behaviour came from France. They were written more than 100 years before Washington was born. They influenced his life and helped shape who he was – as an individual and as the president of the United States.

COMMITMENT TO COMPROMISE

As president of the Constitutional Convention, Washington helped bring together people who had different ideas about the new government. He knew that in order to build a democracy, it was important to find **middle ground**. Despite agreeing with most Federalist ideas, he did not join a political party. Compromise remains an important ideal in politics today. Bipartisanship refers to politicians working together, no matter which party they are from. This can happen if there are very important decisions to make on issues such as foreign policy.

George Washington

THE WIDER PICTURE

Historians recognise that Washington benefited from slavery and his actions harmed many Indigenous peoples. Although he championed democracy and the unity of the nation, he was part of a system that represented white, wealthy, male landowners more than other members of society. Ultimately, Washington is remembered for his role in shaping the presidency, the military and the national identity of the US as we now know it.

Uncovering the Truth
Primary Sources

A lot is known about George Washington and the events of the American Revolution. This is because there are so many primary sources still available to historians today. A primary source is a document or object created at the time of a historical event.

Primary sources include

- official documents
- letters
- diaries
- paintings or drawings
- photographs
- sound recordings
- videos

Photo of original source

DIFFERENT POINTS OF VIEW

Primary and secondary sources may tell different stories depending on the views of the people who created them. A soldier in the British Army would have a different perspective from a soldier in the Continental Army. It is important to question sources – doing this helps us to understand them and understand different perspectives better.

CULPER CODE BOOK

The Culper **code** book is a primary source that shows how the Culper Spy Ring communicated during the revolution and helped America win the war against Britain. In 1778, Washington asked Major Benjamin Tallmadge to organise the Culper Spy Ring. Tallmadge recruited spies who used fake identities to gather details about British military plans in the New York area. He also developed the Culper code book to protect the spy ring and keep their messages secret. The spies used the book's numerical code to send coded messages to Washington's headquarters. The British Army would not have understood this code.

Original source text

A		B		D	
a	1	behalf	62	date	120
an	2	bitter	63	day	121
all	3	bottom	65	dead	122
at	4	bounty	65	do	123
and	5	bondage	66	die	124
art	6	barron	67	damage	125
arms	7	brigade	68	doctor	126
about	8	business	69	dirty	127
above	9	battery	70	drummer	128
absent	10	battalion	71	daily	129
absurd	11	british	72	dispatch	130
adorn	12				
adopt	13				

A battery was not something used to power electronics. Here it is used to describe a group of heavy guns all being kept in the same place.

A battalion is a large group of soldiers, made up of several companies.

The code book used numbers instead of words. For example, the number 72 meant "British".

Look at the code book, then read the transcribed version of the text and answer the questions below.

Quick questions

- What would a message reading "1, 72, 128" mean?
- How would you say "dispatch a doctor above brigade" in a coded message?
- Was it easy to add new code words to the code book?

Discussion questions

- What kind of information do you think the spies were trying to gather?
- What does this document tell you about the people who were working as part of the spy ring?
- What does the code book teach you about warfare?

- A British drummer.
- 130, 1, 126, 9, 68.
- No. The book was handwritten and the book of each spy would have needed to be updated.

Uncovering the Truth

Secondary Sources

A secondary source is a document or object created after the event, or by someone who was not directly involved in the event. Secondary sources can explain or interpret primary sources. They help in understanding an event.

Secondary sources include

- news articles
- books
- media documentaries
- encyclopaedias

Emanuel Leutze was born in Germany in 1816. He moved to the US with his family in 1825 and lived in Philadelphia. Later, he returned to Germany to study art before painting *Washington Crossing the Delaware.*

THE PAINTING

Washington Crossing the Delaware was created by Emanuel Leutze in 1851. It is a secondary source. The painting is very large, measuring 3.7 m (12 ft) in height and 6.4 m (21 ft) in width. It shows an important scene from the American Revolution – George Washington and his troops crossing the icy Delaware River on their way to the Battle of Trenton on Christmas Day, 1776.

In October 1851, *Washington Crossing the Delaware* was displayed at an exhibition in New York where it was viewed by at least 50,000 people. The same year, an American art collector bought it for $10,000, about £338,000 in today's money. This made it very valuable at the time.

Washington Crossing the Delaware

The large chunks of ice help to show how difficult the journey was.

The person standing behind Washington is holding an American flag. It suggests that Washington had the support of America, and that the army is carrying the hopes of the American colonists as they travel.

The soldiers on the boat are working hard to sail across the river, despite the conditions. This emphasises their commitment to the revolution and to Washington himself.

Washington is the tallest figure and one of only two standing in the foreground. He is looking forward and has one leg up on the side of the boat. This shows him as a determined leader, ready for action.

Look at the painting, then read the annotations and answer the questions below.

Quick questions

- Why do you think the artist decided to make the painting so large?
- How does the painting make George Washington the focus?
- What time of year do you think the event happened?

Discussion questions

- Why do you think Emanuel Leutze decided to paint this scene, 75 years after it happened?
- The stars and stripes American flag was not designed until 1777, about six months after the Delaware Crossing. Why do you think the painter decided to include it?
- What was the significance of the Delaware Crossing in the American Revolution?

- The size of the painting emphasises the significance of the event in American history.
- He is shown standing up, is slightly larger than the other people and is in the middle of the painting.
- The ice in the river and the way the soldiers are dressed shows that it happened in winter.

Vocabulary Builder

Long Live Washington!

How might George Washington's inauguration have been reported? Read this fictional article to see how a newspaper might cover the story. Pay attention to key words that describe the event and the mood of the people.

WASHINGTON BECOMES THE FIRST PRESIDENT OF THE UNITED STATES

Early in the morning, crowds gathered outside George Washington's residence. By noon, people had made their way to Federal Hall in New York City to get the best view of this historic moment. The atmosphere was one of excitement and celebration as church bells pealed across the city. Washington was escorted by around 500 soldiers as he travelled in a state coach on his way to become the first president of the United States. Troops fired a 13-gun salute to honour their former commander in chief in a show of respect and admiration. Upon his arrival, people jostled, cheered and waved. Soon, he was seen on the balcony of Federal Hall. As he took the oath of office standing on the balcony, Chancellor Robert Livingston declared, "Long live George Washington, President of the United States!"

Imagine you are reporting on Washington's inauguration for a newspaper. Then use the article on page 42 and the prompts and word bank below to write your own news story.

- **Why is it important?**
- **What are people hoping for?**
- **How do people feel?**

Emotions	nervousness, awe, enthusiasm, joy, jubilation, pride, respect, solidarity, unity
Looking ahead	change, excitement, hope, opportunity, possibilities, transformation, transition, uncertainty, unknown
Governance	accountability, constitution, democracy, duty, federal, independence, liberty, representation, states

Glossary

Agriculture The practice of farming.

Ally Someone who helps and supports someone else.

Articles of Confederation The first written agreement about how the American states should work together before the US Constitution was written.

Authority The power or right to give orders and make decisions.

Breed A group of animals or plants that share certain features and behaviours.

Camp follower Someone who travelled with armies during wars to provide support, such as cooking and nursing.

Cash crop A crop that is grown to sell for profit.

Code Words, letters or symbols that are used in place of others to create secret messages.

Colony An area or region that is governed by another country.

Congress A body of government in the United States charged with discussing ideas and making decisions. It is made up of the Senate and the House of Representatives.

Constitution The written laws that govern a country. The United States has separate constitutions for each state, in addition to the United States Constitution that applies to the entire country.

Continental Army The army formed by American colonists to fight Great Britain.

Declaration of Independence The document that marked the independence of the American colonies from Great Britain and the founding of the United States.

Delegate Someone chosen to represent others, especially at meetings or conferences.

Delegation A group of people who represent a larger group.

Democracy A system of governance where people vote for their leaders.

Discharged To be officially removed from the military.

Elected To be chosen by the public to lead and help make decisions.

Electoral College A group of representatives chosen by each US state to formally elect the president and vice president.

Embarrassed Uneasy, uncomfortable, self-conscious.

Enslaved To be forced to work for someone else without the freedom to stop or leave.

Estate A large area of land owned by one person or group.

Federalist Someone who supported a strong central government during the early years of the United States.

Fertile Land that is rich in nutrients, good for growing things.

Founding Father A leader who helped create the United States and its government.

French and Indian War A war between France and Great Britain fought in North America. It started in 1754 and ended in 1763.

Geometry An area of mathematics that deals with shapes, sizes and space.

Government A group of people who have been given the power to make and enforce laws in a specific area. Everyone who lives in the area must obey these laws.

Hessian A German soldier hired by the British Army during the American Revolution to fight against the colonists.

Historian Someone who studies the past.

Inaugurated To have officially taken office. Presidents are inaugurated in a special ceremony.

Indentured In colonial times, this referred to someone who worked for a set number of years to pay off the cost of something. Many indentured servants worked to pay for the cost of travelling to North America from overseas.

Indigenous Indigenous peoples are groups of people who are the original inhabitants of a region or area. There may be many different groups of Indigenous peoples within a region, each with their own languages and cultures.

Justice The idea that people should be treated fairly by the law.

Memorial Something created to remember a person or event.

Middle ground A compromise.

Militia A military force whose soldiers are civilians. Militias help armies in emergencies.

Morals Principles about what is right and wrong.

Negotiate To discuss something in order to reach an agreement.

Neutral Not taking sides in a disagreement or war.

Obelisk A tall four-sided object that gets smaller as it rises and ends in a pyramid.

Outnumbered To be fewer in number than another group.

Pension A payment that is made regularly to someone either by the government or their former employer when they retire from their job.

Plantation A vast estate where major cash crops like cotton and tobacco were grown.

Planter Someone who managed or owned a large farm or farms.

Posthumous After the death of a person.

Rallying cry A speech or text that causes people to join together to support a cause.

Regiment A military unit.

Relocated To be moved from one place to another.

Republican Party A party founded in 1792 that favoured states' rights. It eventually turned into the modern Democratic Party. Historians refer to it as the Democratic-Republican Party.

Resigned To have voluntarily left a job or position.

Second Continental Congress A meeting of delegates from the American colonies that took place during the American Revolution.

Senate One of the two chambers that make up Congress. Senators represent their states and discuss and vote on important issues there.

Seven Years' War A war fought between most of the European powers from 1756 to 1763. The primary sides were Great Britain and Prussia against France and Austria.

Slavery A system in which people were owned by their enslavers and forced to work without pay.

Source A written document, artefact or building that provides information relating to the past. Sources are also known as evidence.

Supreme Court The highest court in the US justice system. It is made up of nine justices who make decisions on important issues.

Surveyor Someone who measures land to determine its boundaries and features.

Symbol Something that represents something else.

Term A set amount of time that an elected official, such as a president, will stay in office.

Territory An area of land that is owned or claimed by a country or group.

Treaty An official agreement between two or more groups, such as two countries. It states how they will act or what they will do.

Unclaimed To not be taken or owned by anyone.

Unity To come together as one.

Index

Acknowledgments

The publisher would like to thank the following for their kind permission to reproduce their photographs:

(Key: a-above; b-below/bottom; c-centre; f-far; l-left; r-right; t-top)

4 Alamy Stock Photo: North Wind Picture Archives (c); Science History Images (bl). **4–5 Alamy Stock Photo:** IanDagnall Computing (t). **6 Alamy Stock Photo:** North Wind Picture Archives (br). **Getty Images:** Sepia Times (cl). **7 Alamy Stock Photo:** Historical Images Archive (tc); World History Archive (cr). **8 Alamy Stock Photo:** World History Archive (b). **9 Alamy Stock Photo:** Classic Image (b); Historic Images (t). **10–11 Alamy Stock Photo:** Katharine Andriotis (bc). **Bridgeman Images:** Liszt Collection (tc). **11 Alamy Stock Photo:** Antiqua Print Gallery (br); Gado Images (tr). **12 Alamy Stock Photo:** Stock Montage, Inc. (b). **Getty Images:** Culture Club (tr). **13 Alamy Stock Photo:** CBW (t); FromOldBooks.org (c); North Wind Picture Archives (b). **14 Alamy Stock Photo:** North Wind Picture Archives (b). **15 Alamy Stock Photo:** The Granger Collection (br); Lebrecht Music & Arts (tl); Universal Images Group North America LLC (cl). **16 Bridgeman Images:** Matthew Frey / Wood Ronsaville Harlin, Inc. USA (b). **17 Alamy Stock Photo:** Azoor Photo (t); GL Archive (c); Universal Images Group North America LLC (b). **18 Alamy Stock Photo:** Everett Collection Inc (t); Old Paper Studios (b). **19 Alamy Stock Photo:** North Wind Picture Archives (t). Bridgeman Images: Granger (br). **20 Alamy Stock Photo:** FineArt (r). **21 Alamy Stock Photo:** Pictorial Press Ltd (b); Science History Images (tl). **26 Alamy Stock Photo:** Lake Erie Maps and Prints (b). **27 Alamy Stock Photo:** Randy Duchaine (cr); Smith Archive (t). **28 Alamy Stock Photo:** IanDagnall Computing (tc, tl); Niday Picture Library (tr); PRISMA ARCHIVO (b). **29 Alamy Stock Photo:** Ian Dagnall (br); Granger Historical Archive (tr); The Syndicate (cl). **30 Alamy Stock Photo:** Mark Rose (cr); Science History Images (b). **31 Alamy Stock Photo:** Everett Collection Inc (bc); Hi-Story (t); IanDagnall Computing (c); The History Collection (bl). **32 Bridgeman Images:** Peter Newark American Pictures (t). Getty Images: Stocktrek Images (b). **33 Alamy Stock Photo:** GL Archive (t); IanDagnall Computing (c). Getty Images: FPG (b). **34 Alamy Stock Photo:** Chronicle (b); incamerastock (t); imageBROKER.com (c). **35 Alamy Stock Photo:** Sean Pavone (b); Frank Vetere (t). **36 Alamy Stock Photo:** Classic Image (b). **37 Alamy Stock Photo:** Associated Press (t); GL Archive (b). **38 Library of Congress, Washington, D.C.:** George Washington Papers (b). **39 Courtesy of Mount Vernon Ladies' Association:** (t). **40 Alamy Stock Photo:** GL Archive (b). **41 Alamy Stock Photo:** Vidimages (t). **43 Alamy Stock Photo:** North Wind Picture Archives (t).

Cover images: *Front:* **Alamy Stock Photo:** Peter Horree br, North Wind Picture Archives c, Photo 12 t/(background); **Dreamstime.com:** W.scott Mcgill bl; *Back*: **Alamy Stock Photo:** Ian Dagnall b, incamerastock c; **Bridgeman Images:** Liszt Collection tl.

Quote attributions:

Henry, Patrick and Humphrey, Henry E. 1913. *Give Me Liberty, or Give Me Death!* Audio. https://www.loc.gov/item/jukebox-132710/.

All the books in the DK Super History series have been reviewed by authenticity readers to ensure the represented cultures and experiences are accurate.

This book uses language as appropriate to modern contexts. Historical terms that are no longer acceptable may be present in original source materials and images. These sources are included to present authentic insights into history.